BRIGHT NOTES

ALL QUIET ON THE WESTERN FRONT BY ERICH MARIA REMARQUE

Intelligent Education

Nashville, Tennessee

BRIGHT NOTES: All Quiet on the Western Front
www.BrightNotes.com

No part of this publication may be used or reproduced in any manner whatsoever without written permission, except in the case of brief quotations in critical articles and reviews. For permissions, contact Influence Publishers http://www.influencepublishers.com.

ISBN: 978-1-645421-10-8 (Paperback)
ISBN: 978-1-645421-11-5 (eBook)

Published in accordance with the U.S. Copyright Office Orphan Works and Mass Digitization report of the register of copyrights, June 2015.

Originally published by Monarch Press.
Rose Kam; John S. White, 1966
2019 Edition published by Influence Publishers.

Interior design by Lapiz Digital Services. Cover Design by Thinkpen Designs.

Printed in the United States of America.

Library of Congress Cataloging-in-Publication Data forthcoming.
Names: Intelligent Education
Title: BRIGHT NOTES: All Quiet on the Western Front
Subject: STU004000 STUDY AIDS / Book Notes

CONTENTS

1) Introduction to Erich Maria Remarque 1

2) Textual Analysis
   Detailed Analysis 11

3) Character Analyses 30

4) Critical Commentary 43

5) Essay Questions and Answers 63

6) Bibliography 67

INTRODUCTION TO ERICH MARIA REMARQUE

EARLY YEARS

Erich Maria Remarque was born in 1897 in Osnabruck, Westphalia. His family, of French descent, had come to the Rhineland after the French Revolution. In contradiction to later Nazi reports classifying him as a Jew, Remarque was raised a Roman Catholic. He attended the Gymnasium and was drafted into World War I at the age of eighteen. During the ensuing war years, he was wounded five times, on the last occasion seriously.

After the Armistice his first two jobs were teaching, which he hated, and stone-cutting, in his hometown cemetery, which he enjoyed. Later he was a test driver for a Berlin tire company.

Remarque's literary career began with magazine articles and advertising copy. Later, he was assistant editor of Sportbild, an illustrated sports magazine.

HIS FIRST SUCCESS

It was during this assistant-editorship in 1929, that Remarque wrote *All Quiet on the Western Front*. Its launching was not without **irony**. The first publisher approached by Remarque refused the story, and the second accepted with distinct reluctance. Twelve hundred thousand copies were sold in Germany alone. Translations and movie rights made Remarque a rich man and a vulnerable one.

REACTION

A tall blond athletic man, Erich Remarque was built like a halfback. He was a crack mechanic as well as a fine musician. He loved dogs, and was energetic and vivacious in company he liked. But he was shy to the point of avoiding strangers, and hated publicity. His fame actually drove him to retirement to Porto Ronco on Lake Maggiore in Switzerland.

LATER YEARS

Remarque hated Nazism as much as he hated war, and the Nazis retaliated by burning his books and making his exile permanent by depriving him of German citizenship. He came to the United States in 1939 and took up residence in Los Angeles.

OTHER WORKS

Later publications by Remarque include *Arch of Triumph*, *Spark of Life* and *A Time to Love and a Time to Die*. Further information on these works is given in the Bibliography at the end of this study.

BACKGROUND

Germany After World War I

All Quiet on the Western Front was produced against a background of war fatigue and disillusionment in a conquered country gripped by inflation and starvation, a country disillusioned with nearly half a century of Prussian brainwashing that had led it only to this. The German Empire had become a land exhausted by entirely new or terrifyingly improved weapons of war; men had been robbed of all individuality; the age-old military factors of bravery, enterprise, and skill had been rendered meaningless. Men of all nations, on both sides of the conflict, had been reduced, finally, to merely passive recipients of torture.

It was a time when Conservatives, Socialists, and Communists, instead of cooperating to make their new republic a success, sabotaged each other's efforts. Intellectuals paraphrased Nietzsche's Zarathustra to remind the people that their pious obedience to their country had created only the Kaiser and his drill sergeants. Writers took advantage of the floodgate flung open by military defeat to unleash a torrent of abuse and criticism of both patriotism and war itself. No longer were the heroic aspects of battle featured. Instead, the new literature stressed mud and sweat, hunger and thirst, blood, lust, crime, brutality, and destruction. In the end, these authors took refuge in **satire**, or, with their fellow artists, sought escape in the forms of exoticism, expressionism, and dadaism.

To understand such a situation more clearly, it is necessary to review briefly the spirit of Prussianism, so largely its cause, and the nature of those engines of destruction against which this spirit had flung the German people in a war that involved most of the Western world.

Prussianism

Even before the appearance of Bismarck, Prussia had twice appeared as a leading nation, if not the leader, in that multitude of states ruled by feudalism and Church in the land which later came to be known as Germany.

In the years immediately following the Thirty Years' War (1618–1648), while still under the control of the disintegrating Holy Roman Empire, Germany had two ideals: unity and liberty. Hope for the first was seen in the eighteenth century in the House of Hohenzollern. Frederick the Great, by his conquests, by his substitution of the doctrine of service for that of divine right, and by his forty-six years of almost unbroken labor (1740–1786) was an inspiring leader who pointed the way to a modern state. It would be a state in contrast to the dynastic lands of the Hapsburgs, who ruled earlier in its history, and to neighboring nations, festering with idleness. In him was seen a ruler under whom men might become united and for the first time hear the appellation, "German," with honor, affirming a native high culture and a cosmopolitan spirit, combined with a unifying military superstructure.

Imitators of the Prussian monarch sprang up in the German states. George P. Gooch comments, in Germany, that (before Frederick) "Nowhere in Europe was absolutism more repulsive ..." and a satirist is quoted as writing, "The peasant ... is like a sack of meal. When emptied, there is still some dust in it-it only needs to be beaten."

Oddly enough, the first setback in Prussia's rise to eventual power came at a time when the other German ideal, liberty, was first becoming a reality elsewhere. The French Revolution was hailed in Germany, as was Napoleon's conquest of the Holy Roman Empire. But it was that same conqueror who also destroyed the Prussian army. Nevertheless, as Gooch writes, again in Germany, "The years which followed the **catastrophe of Jena (1806)** were a time not only of suffering but of hope." Prussia's defeat by France only strengthened the feeling of nationalism in Germany, and even converted Johann Fichte, who had been one of Germany's most eloquent philosophical advocates of radical cosmopolitanism. In an address to the German nation, Fichte blamed all Germans for their collapse, and urged all to cooperate in reconstruction on a national level.

Again Germans looked to Prussia with their new patriotism and, by cooperating with Austria and Russia for the first time, Prussia justified their hopes. With their combined forces and that of the British, the French were driven from Germany and Napoleon finally was defeated at Waterloo, in Belgium, in 1815.

Prussia's second setback was caused by the contradictory action of its king, Frederick William IV. Where his great grandfather had abandoned divine right for service, he now revived the former doctrine and, in 1849, made it his reason for refusing the emperorship of the Federation of German States offered to him by the Frankfort Parliament. With it he would have had to accept a constitution, and it was against his principles to rule as the will of majorities wished. He believed that princes only, and not the people, could choose their ruler, who must then rule, as Gooch writes, "... in accordance with the law of God ... and his own unfettered discretion." Opportunity did not knock again until the days of Bismarck, when it was fulfilled with "blood and iron."

When William I reconsidered abdication because Count Otto von Bismarck consented to head the Ministry in 1861, not only Germany's fortunes, but those of all of Europe and eventually of the world were to change.

Under his leadership, Austria and then France were to fall before a German war machine headed by the Prussian military. But even Bismarck was to prove unable to control the force he had created. With matchless diplomacy, he had arranged matters so that both Austria and France were without allies when they faced Germany. After the fall of France, however, the military annexed French Lorraine as well as German-born Alsace (1871), a move which is regarded as perhaps the most important mistake in Bismarck's career. It was the French who, toward the end of Bismarck's rule, supported the various divisive elements in the German Empire and who, indeed, agitated stubbornly against political restpoints of the masses and against the friendly relations sought by Bismarck between France and Prussia.

At the time, however, this "victory" was part of the wave of exultation which flooded an area that was once composed of feudal states overrun by war, an area which now had been transformed by a diplomatic genius into an empire. All but a few Germans were content at first to leave rule to a revered Emperor, an adored Crown Prince, and an Iron Chancellor. The people were not to regain a real voice in government for still another 50 years. During that time, Bismarck was to be dismissed by a new emperor (William II, in 1890) whose organized chauvinism was far more deadly than that of the undisciplined Louis Napoleon. Also, in that interval, there was to be another war, which, as Bismarck had prophesied, was to make the one of 1870 seem child's play. This war, of course, was World War I. The age of "blood and iron" was to run away from its creator.

Under the Prussian military, Germans were transformed from poets, thinkers, and dreamers to victorious soldiers. A creed of culture was replaced by a faith in force.

Even before Bismarck, professorial members of the Prussian school had paved the way for imperialism by glorifying the Hohenzollerns as destined leaders. And after the advent of that Chancellor, the most famous member of this school carried its work still further. Professor Heinrich von Treitschke, known as "the Bismarck of the Chair," spoke to all Germans throughout the last quarter of the nineteenth century as he proclaimed the supremacy of power and the State. He argued that peace was immoral, advocated the duel as a training ground for war, and otherwise attempted to promote national military supremacy. So influential was he that he was elected to the Reichstag as early as 1871 and, although he died in 1896, has been accused of being one of the instigators of World War I.

True Prussianism, however, the background of death on the Western Front, was pictured more clearly early in the twentieth century by Professor Hans Delbruck even as he argued, apparently, for democracy. Delbruck thought that placing all power in representatives of the people was as erroneous as giving it all to the autocracy. The first he declared an impossibility, because a true majority could never be ascertained in elections where many never voted. And he cited Jena as proof of the folly of the second. The best government, he asserted, was the dual kind existing in Germany where the Constitution was a balance between Prince and Reichstag. But even Delbruck claimed that real rule lay in military command. And he acknowledged that the loyalty of the Prussian military would always be to their war-lord Emperor rather than to the State. He himself was an officer in the Franco-Prussian War and was so nationalistic that after World War I he attempted to prove that Russia, not Germany, was responsible for its occasion.

Even more influential was Prince Bernhard von Bulow. As recently as the turn of the century, he argued that Germany's central-European position without naturally protective frontiers demanded her existence as a military state. In such a state, he maintained, monarchial guidance was essential.

This then was the foundation of rule by Kaiser and drill sergeants as structured by Prussianism, against which its victims were to rail in Germany after World War I. To quote Gooch, in Germany once again, the country " ... was a glittering vision of mind and muscle, of large-scale organization, of intoxicating self-confidence, of metallic brilliancy such as Europe had never seen. Yet the country was restless, its appetite for power unappeased; and here and there a voice was heard to ask whether it was being led, and what it would profit a nation if it gained the whole world and lost its own soul."

Such were the forces and confusion which brought men to the Front. It now remains to discuss briefly the weapons that destroyed those men, men who, as Remarque states in a simple dedication in his book, "even though they may have escaped its shells, were destroyed by the war."

Weapons Of World War I

Almost immediately after the outbreak of hostilities, there was revealed in World War I a potential for terrifying superiority of material for destruction over the individual will for survival. This reached its climax with the launching of poison gas by Germany and, later, of tanks by the Allies. Each of these comparatively modern weapons, however, will bear individual discussion, along with earlier weapons adapted to modern warfare.

The Machine-Gun

This was the most destructive weapon of World War I. It caused ninety of every one hundred casualties.

The High-Explosive Shell

This missile soon replaced shrapnel during the war. It was effective not only on contact, but also through the action of heat and sound waves.

Trench Mortar and Hand-Grenade

These favorite weapons of castle-besiegers' wars were found very useful in trench warfare.

Tanks

The impotence of men before these irresistible armored giants is perhaps best described in *All Quiet on the Western Front* itself.

Anti-Tank Rifles

These 35-pound weapons required two men for firing but were seldom used; so great was the fear inspired by tanks that the rifles were virtually ineffective.

Liquid Fire

This was first used by the French in the Argonne in 1914. Germans argued that nothing, including poison gas, could have been more inhumane.

Poison Gas

No weapon unleashed in mankind's wars aroused such a reaction of fury as did poison gas, first used by the Germans on April 22, 1915, during the second battle of Ypres. Strangely, this reaction was not caused by the actual harm inflicted. Although the effect of the gas in itself was very tortuous, it certainly was no more cruel than the living cremation of the flame thrower, nor more effective on the human body than high explosives. What actually aroused bitter anger and outrage was the feeling of impotence engendered before the protection of masks was devised. As C. F. Crutwell writes in *A History of the Great War 1914–1918*: "In the face of gas, without protection, individuality was annihilated; the soldier in the trench became a mere passive recipient of torture and death. A final stage seemed to be reached in the whole tendency of modern scientific warfare to depress and make of no effect individual bravery, enterprise, and skill."

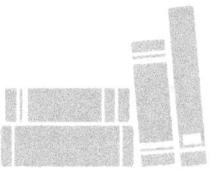

ALL QUIET ON THE WESTERN FRONT

TEXTUAL ANALYSIS

DETAILED ANALYSIS

CHAPTER ONE

A short distance behind the German front lines, eighty survivors of recent trench warfare get an unexpected break. They receive food and tobacco rations intended for 70 company members who didn't return with them from the last fourteen-days' engagement. A cowardly cook's mean reluctance to allow the extra food is overruled by a lieutenant who had been promoted from the ranks.

Conversation turns to a letter received from Kantorek, a former school master, whose orated platitudes had influenced the enlistment of these nineteen-year-old boys. The storyteller, Paul Baumer, now regards Kantorek as a betrayer, since he had been trusted and respected and should never have guided pupils into fighting in a war which youth now knows as the elderly never will. The chapter closes with a visit to Kemmerich, a dying comrade, in the dressing station. They keep their knowledge of his condition from him, and Paul uses cigarettes to bribe an orderly to dope the sufferer. But Muller, another of their group, already starts maneuvers to be there at the death. He wants Kemmerich's boots.

Comment

In *All Quiet on the Western Front*, Remarque has been praised for power and characterization even as he was been criticized for sensationalism, brutality, and lack of selection. As the story develops, it tends to support the last three charges, but little justification for them can be found in the opening chapter. Realistic, it certainly is, but that in itself no longer constituted sensationalism in the twentieth century. Long before, Stephen Crane had set a contrasting pattern to the romantic school of war novels which preceded *The Red Badge of Courage*. At the time of that novel's publication, Crane himself might have been called sensational for picturing the type of soldier who, later, at a rally, was to toast all those who, like himself, ran at Shiloh. Since then, however, enough **realism** has appeared in literature to prevent the appellation of "sensationalist" to a writer who merely does not wince from admitting the roles of rats and lice in history.

It is true that Remarque's description of the dying Kemmerich in the dressing station is an example of additive detail characteristic of the naturalism that so often is branded brutal and sensational. So too does the element of determinism, which placed these boys here, mark him as a naturalist. Still, in this chapter, at least, there is a selection which confines that kind of writing to a portrayal of the dressing station, where, even in romantic war stories, surgeons carried on the grimmest work of all, and which, as depicted by Remarque, is quite revealing to those who have never been in one.

On the other hand, the favorable quality of characterization is evident almost from the start. In a minimum of words, the analytical Kropp, the intellectually befogged Muller, and the bearded Leer all appear vividly. So too do the ever-skinny Tjaden of perpetual appetite, the huge-handed Westhus, and Katczinsky, who could never be mistaken for anything but a farmer. Indeed, Remarque's characterization becomes even national. German youth is seen as more physically disciplined but more intellectually rebellious than ours. These soldiers do not try to rationalize fear upon the grounds of superior officers' incompetence, as did the Civil War ones in Crane's novel. But they do blame those who were their scholarly mentors, and thus reflect the academic freedom of thought which once permitted a German undergraduate to tell his professor that the latter's statements were not in accordance with actuality.

CHAPTER TWO

After reflecting briefly on the completeness with which war can cut off a youth from the past if it snatches him before the stages of life-work, marriage, and children, Paul recollects his days of training. He remembers the senselessness of the whole system in general and the tyranny of one noncommissioned officer in particular. He, Kropp, Tjaden, and Westhus were special targets of little Corporal Himmelstoss, and were given tasks as inconceivable as they were humiliating. Here, however, their youth, which was a handicap in many respects, came to their rescue. It enabled them to endure instead of cracking, and to develop a tough viciousness which alone prevented insanity after they entered trench warfare.

Paul is at Kemmerich's bedside when the latter dies. Returning with Kemmerich's boots, he gives them to Muller.

Comment

In the middle of this chapter, we find an excellent example of **exposition**, one of the four chief types of composition. Narration and description are blended with it to give the reader a clear idea of the nature and operation of one phase of the German military machine. This **exposition** is particularly interesting to those against whom it was launched in two World Wars. Many preconceived ideas are found to be true; but others not altogether so. We learn that even in the German Army a noncommissioned officer was not without fear of what truths a private might reveal at a hearing. Also we find that German officers can be offended at senselessly inhuman disciplinary tactics, even as they can be amused by retaliation within the rules.

Even as Paul's account of basic training constitutes excellent **exposition**, so do we find examples of argumentation in his opening reflections and powerful description at the end.

Already the purpose of this novel seems to be not only a revelation of the incomprehensible horrors of war but also that of its particularly devastating effect upon youth. Hardened as Paul has already been by both preparation and war itself, he still feels the need to justify Muller's desire for the boots. He is quick to reveal Muller's willingness to walk unshod upon barbed wire, could such action have helped Kemmerich. But, that not being the case, he can only cite the one remaining reality of fact with regard to the boots and praise Muller's ability to see that fact clearly.

Additive detail is employed again to some extent in the closing death scene, but the literary power which brings the reader with Paul to the dying man's side comes not only from the pictured stages of life's exit from Kemmerich's face, it springs also from the impatient businesslike glances shot by overworked orderlies at the cot so soon to become available.

CHAPTER THREE

The chapter opens with an example of Katczinsky's almost miraculous talent for finding useful things where all others swear they can't possibly be. He is portrayed as continuing to search for what is needed even when the others no longer hope. He finds soft straw, warm bread, horse meat, without explanation. Then conversation switches back to training camps and the misuse of power by those who possess it there. As usual the special subject is Himmelstoss. An especially humiliating abuse of power on his part is described, and then Paul relates how revenge became sweet on their last day of training. On that occasion he and his friends ambushed the little corporal, threw a sheet over his head, and then administered a severe beating.

Comment

Again the **theme** is the effect of military training upon men. It permits those in authority to reveal their truly animal nature which civilian life compels them to conceal. Also, the victims learn their lessons too well. The humiliating techniques of Himmelstoss were thoroughly mastered by those against whom they were employed; and the result was a punishment inflicted upon the corporal which was as degrading as it was severe.

Also, in this chapter, there appears justification for the accusation that Remarque will shock in order to impress, even as Whitman did in his earlier days. The novelist, however, has a more valid defense than the poet, who could never claim to come nearer to **realism** than the transition stage between that form of writing and earlier romanticism. As a realist, Remarque has the right to select those details whose description will give the truest picture. Admittedly, it is equally true that such unpleasant incidents need not always be selected to accomplish this. However, a military training camp run under the Prussian regime would probably abound more in the kind of incidents described by a Remarque than a Howells, for example. But, to face the facts, so all-important to Muller, war calls for vicious, not lovable, characteristics, and it is the vicious side of a soldier that is apt to be nurtured and developed. The reader should remember, too, that a good part of Remarque's intent was to highlight the ugliness that was intrinsic to the war and its machinery. If not revealed, this ugliness would be as forgotten as the men who experienced it; it would be as if the war, the men, and their horrible experiences never existed for those people who did not participate directly. Although all mankind knew of World War I, only its soldiers knew its terrible cruelty and horror.

CHAPTER FOUR

Going up to the Front on wiring fatigue with Paul and others, Katczinsky hears the British artillery at an unusually early hour and predicts a bombardment. He is soon proved right, but they continue to a wood, and start wiring. Finished, they await the trucks, but on their way back to meet them, they find themselves literally in the middle of the shelling. A graveyard proves a temporary refuge, but then comes a gas attack, and they are forced to seek higher ground. One of their companions, a young recruit, is so seriously wounded that Paul and Kat are on the verge of a mercy-killing when stretcher bearers appear. The chapter ends with a rain-swept journey on lorries back to the huts, amidst a background of bombardment.

Comment

In this chapter some justification is found for claims from England and Sweden, as well as from Germany, that *All Quiet on the Western Front* is the greatest book ever written. Impressionism, symbolism, naturalism, even mysticism are all employed to create a scene of terror and horror in which the reader participates through the characters. Contrast and **simile** are also used. The incidents range from humiliating physical weakness to almost unbelievably superhuman capacity to care for others when every animal instinct shrieks for self-preservation. We see Paul, comforting and understanding to a boy at a moment of unavoidable shame. We also see him, a short time later, suggesting that he or Kat kill the same boy as an act of mercy.

Although there is a detailed naturalism in the described death agonies of the horses, even here, as in most other places throughout the chapter, Remarque is, above all, impressionistic. He describes not the material itself but the effect it has upon others, and thus leads the reader to discover, see, hear, and feel with them. We realize the roughness of the terrain through the jolting truck and the imminence of the Front through the emotional responses in the characters. In the case of the horses, horror comes as much through the frenzied reaction of Detering and the muffled hearing of the others as it does from direct detailed description. Detering's helpless comment about the wounded horses in their agony, "like to know what harm they've done," maintains the focus of Remarque's theme.

Symbolism is also employed here in mystic writing, not seen to this extent until now. The Front is a whirlpool, and the earth a sustaining force that becomes almost a mother to one of her physically most helpless children. Even air is given life as it is sought by Paul and his companions when they are attacked by poison gas and as it streams into them "like cold water" when the attack is over and they remove their masks.

CHAPTER FIVE

Himmelstoss has finally been sent to the Front after one of his training camp victims proved to be the son of an important townsman. He now approaches his former pupils, only to be alternately ignored and insulted. Attempts by him to have them punished draw a "chewing out" of himself by the company commander and the lightest of sentences for them.

Before and after his appearances, conversations center upon life after the war, and other former students agree that prospects will be bleak for them. The chapter ends with the theft of a goose by Paul and Kat, followed by a hearty meal.

Comment

Modern educators would have been delighted with the conversation about the "Old School." It revealed that accumulation of useless facts which left the pupil utterly unprepared for life, and which has been a bane since Dewey advocated learning by doing.

Considered in connection with the main **theme** of this novel, however, it is less delightful. We are reminded again that war's impact upon youth snatched from schools is devastating. Even if it does not destroy them physically, its psychological effect could prevent them from ever succeeding again in the kind of senseless studies they had left. Too mature for school, they would also find themselves too old to catch up with those already skilled in trade and launched in jobs. They would truly be a lost generation.

Through narration of the Himmelstoss incident, we again learn something about the German army. It has improved. Soldiers are no longer tied to trees in punishment. They are now treated quite like men.

Also in this chapter, we see how the characters of a novel are changed and developed by the action of the plot. Paul, the student, and Katczinsky, the farmer, who wouldn't have had a common thought in previous civilian life, are now closer than brothers. Also, they are partners in the theft of livestock, something that would have been incredible to one and an anathema to the other before the war.

CHAPTER SIX

The continual sound of transports bringing reinforcements to the enemy lines and the sight of fresh coffins prepared for casualties do nothing to raise the morale of the German soldiers as they go up to the Front. Each knows what a tremendous factor uncontrollable luck will play in their survival or destruction. They are especially reminded of this when their own weakened artillery begins to drop shells upon them. Nevertheless, the first days are spent in battling rats and overhauling bayonets.

Then comes a gas attack, but the expected offensive does not follow. The Germans think they may be lucky enough not to have one. This optimism vanishes when a continual bombardment is launched, but there still is no invasion, except from rats. However, expected food cannot reach them. Finally the enemy shells begin to fall behind them, and they know the foe will charge. They pile out of their trenches to meet them.

The enemy advance continues through thrown grenades, machine-gun fire, and grenades left behind in retreat, their fuses pulled to create a mine field. Germans are pushed back into rear trenches, only to pile out again in counter-attack as the enemy falters, then retreats. They drive him in hand-to-hand fighting back through their own recently evacuated trenches, and into the enemy's. There, they pause long enough to snatch provisions, then retreat into their original position. The end of battle finds them too exhausted to eat.

Attack and counterattack follow, interspaced with calm, still memories, which awake no desire for a past these veterans now know to be gone forever. Free time is also devoted to hopeless attempts to teach recruits, utterly unqualified for trench warfare in all respects save courage. Finally they are relieved, and Paul's company, once numbering a hundred and fifty men is now reduced to thirty-two.

Comment

The same meaningless **theme** of attack and counterattack, described sardonically by Stephen Crane in *The Red Badge of Courage*, is portrayed in this chapter by Remarque. Here, however, the engines of destruction are so tremendous that even the bitterest smile is impossible. Also, both writers employ the same technique in another way. Each picture disconnected segments, and not the whole, only an illusion of which is given through a fixed point of vision. But Remarque's results are even greater. Victims are portrayed in detailed agony by Crane, but against a background of the living. The reader who experiences the hell of Front warfare through Paul, however, is as unconvinced as he that anyone has survived.

Here again we see an example of how an illusion of total horror can be created from descriptions of varied incidence. A heaving dugout and a mad recruit! Walls plastered with splinters, flesh, and uniforms, or shrieking soldiers striking out blindly at inrushing rats! These are the incidents chosen by an impressionist to create an effect far greater than the component parts.

Even as Remarque's writing, like Crane's, is an example of impressionism, so does it resemble the American's in its use of contrast for effect. The quietness of the recollected cathedral appearing and dissolving in the light of star shells are particular examples.

CHAPTER SEVEN

Behind the lines, where their dismembered company awaits reinforcements, Paul and his companions encounter French girls, who come along the bank while the men are swimming in the river. Promises of provisions insure welcome, and they swim the river to visit the girls' house, since they cannot cross the bridge without being caught. After two nights of this, Paul gets leave. With the girl, Paul had tried to imagine that a woman was worth fighting for, that the War had some meaning after all. But he told her of his leave and she was disinterested. From her point of view, the bread he had brought was more important than never seeing him again.

At home, all save his invalid mother irritate him with incessant talk about a war they don't understand. Far worse, however, is his growing realization that the past has slipped away forever. Only the sight of his former schoolmaster, Kantorek, now a Territorial, being belittled by one of Paul's classmates, lightens the dejection.

Comment

Here we fully understand the author's own description of this book. He wished neither to accuse nor exalt. His only purpose was to write of men who were destroyed by war, even though they survived physically.

Paul sensed this impending destruction earlier. We have seen evidence of this on many occasions, including his feelings of betrayal by his elders and his own sneering descriptions of past education in which he was joined by fellow pupils. Another was his realization of the lack of family or vocational ties to the life he has left but which he must rejoin should he survive. Even more telling, however, are the almost incredible psychological adaptations, developments of which he realizes, but effects of which he has not foreseen until now. Boys in the trenches, still in their teens, have, by almost superhuman control, banished all feelings, even all thoughts. Were they to permit themselves either, insanity would follow instantly. What they cannot realize in the trenches is the terrible accelerated maturity which accompanies such development, and which will close, in civilian life, the doors of companionship with either contemporaries or their seniors. Only leave brings this home to Paul. The routine of living has been reduced to nothing more than fierce machinery of disciplined, basic survival, with no purpose beyond that.

CHAPTER EIGHT

His long leave over, Paul is given four weeks' duty at a training camp on the moors, instead of being sent back immediately to the Front. There his time is divided between company drill and guarding Russians in an adjoining prison camp. Quite a number of routine training-camp scenes are amply described, all pointing to the personal humiliation of war-time living.

He is also visited there by his father and elder sister, who bring bad news that his mother will have to face an operation for her cancer.

Comment

Remarque insists that his book is an indictment of no one, yet here he uses his powers of description and impressionistic selection to condemn the senseless cruelty of war as powerfully as he had in other chapters, where his weapons were detailed **realism** and shock.

In the days of the romantic war novels which preceded Crane in this country, the two-way degradation of the prison camp was public knowledge, if not the subject of literature. The two reactions of those who visited it were detailed, horrified descriptions of its filth, and expressed conviction of guilt and punishment sure to be inflicted upon those who permitted it.

Remarque's reaction is neither. But, he uses the prison camp itself as a point of vision which creates a total illusion of the incomprehensible insanity of war.

His use of description as he does this meets the standards of literature. It has purpose, is brief but powerful, and employs contrasts. Mainly, however, his total illusion of the terrifyingly humiliating manner in which war can break men is accomplished through description of apparently disconnected incidents.

Contrast is seen in the slinking, cringing movements of big bearded Russians even as it is in the peaceful natural beauty of the moor on which men train for the brutal action of mechanized war. Color, softness, even a ghostlike quality of moving shadow, are the background for loud commands and the panting of running and falling men.

Most powerful of all, however, are the disjointed incidents of earlier intrigues and flashing knives followed by grubbing around garbage and the hopeless bargaining sessions in which food is silently held before starving eyes until all resistance is broken down. It is through these that we experience with Paul a completed picture of the degradation of men who are enemies as a result of a signature at some distant table and who could be made friends by another such signature.

CHAPTER NINE

Paul returns to the trenches in time to be present when the Kaiser inspects troops. Then he volunteers for patrol and is trapped in "No-Man's land."

When a French soldier stumbles into his shell-hole, Paul strikes out instantly with his knife, inflicting a mortal wound. Then, for hours, he is compelled to occupy the shell-hole with his victim, first a dying man, then a corpse. During that time Paul almost loses his mind as he babbles apologies and promises of reparation to the dead man whose pocketbook identifies him as Gerard Duval, a printer.

With the coming of night, protective darkness reawakens the will to live in Paul, and he makes his way back to his own trench. There, his friends talk him out of shock.

Comment

In this chapter, the age-old question of conscripted civilian soldiers is raised again. How did they get there? Paul had wondered about it in the quiet night on the moors as he watched the Russian prisoners. Now it is asked again in the trenches after the Kaiser's inspection. The attempted answers are samples of that savage humor which is the front-line soldier's defense against insanity. They are futile but there is even less answer to the rebuttals. How can a German mountain offend a French mountain? Why should any worker care whether his government is offended when all it means in any country is a combination of police and taxes? If the reasons don't apply to tramps, then may the tramps go home? A good many of the group do not feel themselves offended by the enemy government, nor by the individuals who comprise the enemy army. The reason for the individual's presence in the war is in question.

Another phenomenon puzzling to Paul in the preceding chapter also becomes too terrifyingly personal here. How can a stranger's signature suddenly make the worst crime in civilization the civilized man's highest objective? Or can it?

Paul kills a man. He does not even wait to see whether he is attacked before he stabs. That far-off potentate's signature has made him assume he will be attacked. But that distant signer is not beside him offering any explanation as he sits in a shell-hole and watches a French printer, husband, and father, whom he has never known, die by his own hand.

Only the instinct of self-preservation makes mental survival possible until he reaches his own trench. There he is cured completely as he watches German snipers competing in homicide for medals and promotion.

CHAPTER TEN

A comparatively easy job falls to Paul and his friends. They are ordered to guard an abandoned village and its not-yet-emptied supply dump. For a time they live almost gaily with food and equipment they have confiscated unofficially. Then they are sent out to evacuate a village. On this mission, Paul and Albert Kropp are wounded. Placed on a troop train they finally reach the hospital. There Paul is healed, but Albert's leg is amputated. Throughout, the details of the events are graphically described and personalized for each of the characters.

Comment

The ultimate horror of war is the war hospital; there were hundreds of thousands of them in Germany, in France, and in Russia between 1914 and 1918. Nowhere in this book is the reader's identification with the characters so complete. In the nightmare world of the Front, never experienced by most readers, the author has to use **realism**, naturalism, impressionism, contrast, and every literary device to bring about such identification. Not so here.

Too many readers, as hospital patients, have experienced the state of helplessness during which a doctor could have talked them into submitting to any kind of operation. Fortunately, civilian doctors are not so sanguinary or experimentally curious as were those German war-hospital surgeons with their numerous patients, during a time when personal concern was nearly impossible.

It is doubtful that the detailed naturalistic descriptions of the wounded horses or the phantom agonized cries of the lost victim in "No-Man's land" have the power to make readers cringe as much as the simple flat-footed soldier who would face a life of clubbed feet and a crutch if he says, "Yes," to the inefficient but importunate chief surgeon who is urging an operation. And we know that he probably will, if only out of desperate pain and hopelessness.

Not that Remarque doesn't employ detailed naturalism and contrast to bring home horror here as elsewhere. Description of the different kinds of wounds afford an example of the first. The constant kindness of the nuns, emphasizing as it does the horror and callousness amid which they work, illustrates the second.

CHAPTER ELEVEN

Paul recounts the events of the last terrible year of the war. Detering deserts, is captured and is heard about no more. Berger receives a fatal wound while trying to find and kill a wounded messenger dog. Muller dies in agony after being shot in the stomach with a Verey light. The company commander, Bertinck, dies as he shoots down one of two soldiers who are trying to spout fire from the flame thrower into the oil soaked crater in which his men have taken refuge. In the same engagement, Leer is struck and quickly bleeds to death. Finally, Kat is wounded in the leg. Paul carries him back to the dressing-station unaware that during the last stage of their agonizing trip, Kat has caught a tiny fatal splinter in the head. Upon arrival, Paul realizes he has lost his last friend.

Comment

Only one more experience awaits Paul. He has lost youthful illusions, youth itself, all possibility of resuming his former life, even the capacity to feel or think as a civilized man. The war and its persistent demands have forced voluntary degeneration from the intellectual to the primitive; and Paul has seen his friends, one by one, killed or crippled. There can be but one more event and, so artistic has been the gradual unfolding of the scenes and stages in this tragedy, one feels that that event will occur in the short final chapter.

Again, through Paul as a point of vision, we see defeat as a whole. Starvation, disease, betrayal by profiteers, worn-out weapons, and overwhelming odds are everywhere. And, adding to it all, the **irony**, to the reader at least, that the war was almost at an end. Force and clarity are added here by the author's rhetorical device of repetition as he reiterates the phrase "Summer of 1918" These are, indeed, the final moments of the war!

CHAPTER TWELVE

This last brief chapter finds Paul recuperating from gas poisoning and convinced that armistice is coming soon; but he feels little hope for his generation in the future. He is the last of the seven fellows from his class. The older men who shared his experience will return to their former life bound by ties he never had. The younger, who were never out here, will shove the former soldiers aside in their lack of knowledge of destruction. Nevertheless, Paul is ready to face the future, hoping that the life remaining within him will see him through. Still, he wonders what life can be worth living after all the experiences of war. In the end, it will all be ruin again.

The narrative point of view then changes to the third person, describing how Paul fell on an October day so uneventful that it was described in a communique as, "*All Quiet on the Western Front.*" Paul's face was calm, as though he were glad that the end had come at last.

Comment

The bitter **irony** that was Stephen Crane's, the savage humor that was the soldier's salvation in trench warfare, both are Remarque's, personally, as he closes his story of a generation destroyed by war. The destruction is indeed two-fold, so that our feeling is almost one of relief at Paul's comparatively peaceful end. It was at least a climactic end to an incredible existence and far more merciful than the interminable disintegration which Paul had anticipated would have been. Remarque seems to say in these last few pages that the chances for recreating a useful generative life were altogether non-existent. Too much death, violence, cruelty, and ugliness had been seen or experienced, despite Paul's original strength. Finally, only the slightest impulse to live remained. Should that be extinguished, all the better. Only that impulse, no greater hope, carried Paul through, virtually to the war's end.

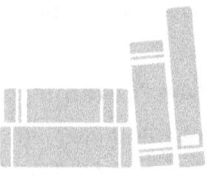

ALL QUIET ON THE WESTERN FRONT

CHARACTER ANALYSES

Paul Baumer

Paul is the narrator and **protagonist** of this story. Set down in the chain of World War I's destructive events, which gradually extinguish him, we see in him a development of the natural strength which made his comrades' mothers turn to him as their offsprings' protector. Courageous, intellectual, and self-controlled, he refuses, almost incredibly, to break under accumulated horror, but his analytical intelligence forces him to realize his inevitable doom, regardless of physical survival. While others, of less sensitivity and intelligence, might cherish the life that remained for them, Paul, by the end of the war had become totally disillusioned.

Franz Kemmerich

Franz is Paul's classmate. His death in the dressing station is a subject of detailed, intimate, realistic writings, sensitive to human sensibilities. He is especially youthful even for his nineteen years. Although a former athlete, approaching death has given him a transparent childlike quality that makes Paul, although already hardened to scenes of death, rage inwardly at the senseless cruelty of war. He is the first of Remarque's characters to play a part, though briefly, in creating an indictment of war's destruction of the individual.

Muller

He is another of Paul's schoolmates. He still clings to their former world of books, a world in which Paul now recognizes the mentors as betrayers. Despite Muller's lingering obsession even here in the trenches, with such things as future examinations and the laws and theories of physics, he is still realistic enough to maneuver for the inheritance of Kemmerich's boots. This apparent callousness, which can make a dying comrade's boots the most important aspect of his death, in another terrifying phenomenon of the Front made real for us by the author.

Stanislaus Katczinsky

"Kat" is the unofficial leader of Paul's group and the object of the narrator's admiration and affection. He is a character who contributes almost as much as the action itself in this story of how the **protagonist** is changed by war. Acute, resourceful, toughened, Kat is a farmer. He has no half-finished play at home, nor any shelf filled with books purchased with ill-spared money or borrowed from friends who are still awaiting their return. Yet his character makes him closer and more admirable to Paul-potential playwright and scholar-than the latter's teachers, classmates, or even relatives. The former peasant, turned poacher and thief by war, has replaced the professor in the chain of people and events which is shaping Paul and his views.

Corporal Himmelstoss

Himmelstoss is a despicable little tyrant who has command of Paul and some of the other schoolmates at the training camp. Better known as the "Terror of Kosterberg," he typifies the degradation of the Prussian military system, which had as an objective the transformation of men into beasts. Yet, the victims themselves admitted that some of this transformation was necessary if soldiers were to maintain sanity at the front. Because of this, Himmelstoss may be regarded as an instrument of the Prussian machine and an example of its success; hence, a victim of that machine, without humanity or personality.

Albert Kropp

He is the clearest thinker of Paul's group. More than that, he is the central figure in one of the most unbearable realistic **episodes** of the story. Just as Kemmerich was the object of focus in the impressionistic portrayal of the dressing station, so Kropp occupies a similar role in the scene in the hospital where his leg is amputated. The central **theme** there, if we can point to one, is Paul's fear that the uncompromising Kropp will shoot himself, as he has promised, should his leg be cut off. He is also a leading voice in discussions among the group, clear-headed, reasonable, intelligent and realistic.

Kantorek

Paul's former schoolmaster, he is a typical product of the Prussian nationalism which first made Germany great, then plunged her into a World War, now known to be lost already, in the first days of 1914, when the British Admiralty ordered out the blockade. Nationalistic and blood-thirsty, he persuaded Paul and his companions to enlist. Later, as his world is vanishing with approaching defeat, he is a ridiculous and humiliated figure in the training camp.

Heinrich

Also known as Ginger, Heinrich is a red-headed, cowardly cook who won't bring his kitchen near enough to the front lines so that the soldiers can have hot food. He is also inherently stingy. The opening incident in this story is an excellent example of how the course of narrated action can spring from the nature of someone's character. Ginger's purely selfish unwillingness to divide one hundred and fifty rations among eighty survivors is the single cause of the action here. Through him, too, a number of other characters are given their initial descriptions.

Lieutenant Bertinck

Bertinck is Paul's company commander. An excellent front-line officer who has risen from the ranks, he is a contrast to the arrogant degrading Prussian militarists who treat men like beasts. Just and knowledgeable, on the one hand, he reprimands Himmelstoss for his former humiliating abuse of authority and on the other, he looks the other way when Paul pummels the corporal for cowardice. The manner in which he dies is suitable to the characteristic concern he shows for his men. His death wound is received even as he kills one of the two soldiers who are trying to ignite the oil-soaked crater in which Bertinck's men have taken refuge with flame throwers.

The Major

He is a typically arrogant product of old-line Prussianism. He humiliates Paul for not saluting when on leave and typifies the cause for mutiny which seized the German army in the last days of the war.

The German Master

One of Paul's former teachers, like Kantorek, he continues to live in a world that is dead, but doesn't know it. Although he and his companions refer to Paul as the "Young Warrior" and shower him with drinks and cigars, they are sure that they know much more about the war than he does.

Tjaden

Tjaden is a skinny young locksmith. He is the biggest eater in Paul's company. In one incident, at least, he is also an example of how a literary artist like Remarque can present a conventional, yet entertaining, character. A completely uneducated non-intellectual, Tjaden breaks up an intellectual conversation about the cause of wars by the unanswerable elemental directness of his questions. "Tramps," such as he, need not be involved in causes or wars. As a common person, he has no use and no purpose in such things.

A Little Brunette

One of the French girls in the house across the river which Paul and his companions visit; she remains nameless. She is another character used by Remarque to illustrate how far the causes of war are from those individuals who are fighting it and from those who are not. The girl's simple point seems to be that she is sorry for soldiers of either side, but she welcomes them and the provisions they bring, that humanity and hunger are basic and uncomplicated by uniform markings.

Detering

This man is another farmer, with thoughts only for his wife and his crops. Even in the front lines he worries about the weather at home. Paul has envied him because he at least will have something to which he can return. But the sight of a white cherry tree in bloom is the point at which Detering snaps. The call of his farm suddenly becomes too great. He deserts and is captured. His comrades do not hear of him again.

Mrs. Baumer

Paul's mother, she is dying of cancer. Mrs. Baumer is unable to picture life at the front, but she is the most understanding of all at home and **refrains** from asking questions. She seems to sense that if a soldier talked about the terror of such things, he would no longer be able to master them.

Gerard Duval

Gerard Duval is a French soldier who is stabbed to death when he drops at night into the shell-hole where Paul has sought refuge from him. Paul kills him instinctively, merely stabbing in the dark at the unknown intruder. The very anonymity of this man, no longer alive because of him, increases for Paul the horror of his act. It becomes worse when Paul learns the harmless facts of his life from the dead man's purse. Duval was a printer, a husband, a father, the kind of man whom Paul probably would have liked. Now, the insanity of war has made Paul his murderer. Paul goes almost insane before lessening fire permits him to leave the shell-hole.

Leer

Another of Paul's classmates, he possesses a full beard, an excellent mathematical mind and prefers girls from officers' brothels. A companion of Paul's on that visit to the little brunette and her friends in the house across the river, Leer makes a great hit with the blonde member of the group. Leer is killed by a piece of shrapnel; in describing the scene, Paul cannot help remarking how little help are Leer's mathematical: talents he bleeds to death within two minutes.

Haie Westhuis

A former peat digger who can conceal a ration loaf in his hand, he is also Kat's strong-arm man on food gathering expeditions. He was also one of the chastisers of Himmelstoss when that unfortunate corporal finally learned that he had succeeded too well in transforming boys into vengeful animals.

Bulcke

Bulcke is a cook at the First Company. This character is an illustration of Remarque's frequent use of contrast to strengthen impression. Fat and courageous, he emphasizes Ginger's cowardice by bringing his equipment right up to the front line, while Ginger would not.

Hans Kramer, Martens, Myer, Beyer, and Hammerling

These are members of Paul's company. They are killed in the attack and counterattack which tore men to bits, laid bodies open for other men to fall into them, and gained not an inch for either side. The description of their deaths is tersely gruesome, but even grimmer is the philosophy forged by war which makes their friends dismiss them with an indifferent shrug as dead and, therefore, no longer important to the living.

Josef Behm

Plump and homely, Behm was a classmate of Paul's who didn't want to enlist. That he did so was due to the lecturing and personal shepherding of Kantorek. Oddly enough, Behm was one of the first to fall. Struck in the eye, blind, and maddened by pain, he couldn't find cover before another fatal bullet found him. Yet this character creates action even after he is dead. When Kantorek becomes a Territorial and meets a former pupil, Mittelstadt now a superior officer, he is reminded that but for him, Behm would have had at least two more months to live until the draft. Mittelstadt also further humiliates Kantorek during training. In life Behm was a victim of the militant nationalism which pervaded even academic life in Germany. After death, he affords us a preview of the postwar disillusionment with Prussianism which was to grip that country.

Wolf

Wolf is a trainee who died of inflammation of the lungs during the inhuman ordeals of training camp. Such a character, although he plays no part in creating the story, is used to indict a system. As long as there is war demanding the hard, pitiless, vicious, and tough, so must there be training camps to develop such qualities. In miniature, Wolf is a victim of a system even as was Melville's *Billy Budd*. Impressment in the British Navy demanded such officers as Master-at-Arms John Claggart, who resembled, more than anything else, sadistic jailors, whose cruelties could not be avenged while the system responsible for them prevailed.

Heinrich Bredmeyer

Bredmeyer is a soldier and fellow townsman of Paul's who has come home first and disturbed Paul's mother with descriptions of the Front. Here again is an example of how action involving one participant in a story can spring from the character of another. Presumably inherently tactless, Bredmeyer is a character who acts rather than is acted upon in the plot-and Paul's leave becomes increasingly difficult to enjoy.

Mittelstadt

This is the former classmate of Paul's who has the pleasure of ordering their old schoolmaster, Kantorek, about of training camp. In this case the character does not create the story but is changed by it. Formerly Kantorek was a figure of menace who held Mittelstadt's whole future in his hands. His offer then to use his influence in connection with examinations would have seemed an unbelievable answer to hopeless prayers. Now, with the knowledge gained in two years of war that survival for any kind of examination is most unlikely, Mittelstadt sneers at what would have been Kantorek's most powerful weapon. In the new world, the Commander, not the headmaster, is all important, and the Commander has no time for teachers. Kantorek has become something too useless for thought, let alone worry.

Erna

Paul's oldest sister, she is the first to greet him upon his return during leave. She also informs him of his mother's cancer, but otherwise has no role in the story.

Boettchner

Boettchner is a porter at Paul's school who later becomes as good a trainee as Kantorek, the headmaster, is a bad one. Nothing so emphasizes the change that gripped Germany as the scene where the porter is held up to the headmaster as an example of good learning.

Mrs. Kemmerich

Franz Kemmerich's mother, she typifies the weeping hysterical mother, mourning her dead son, just as Mrs. Baumer portrays the silent suffering type. No realistic picture of war's grim story would be complete without either.

A Russian Violinist

He is an otherwise anonymous prisoner whose playing is the subject of beautiful descriptive writing in Chapter Eight.

Sergeant Oellrich

A sniper who is pointed out to Paul as Kat and Albert Kropp try to bring Paul back to normalcy after the killing of the French printer, Duval. Oellrich and others are zealously competing in homicide, and he is ahead. The sergeant punctuates his shooting with descriptions of how his human targets jumped when hit. Kat reminds Paul that Oellrich will be decorated or promoted if he keeps this up, and Paul recovers from his shock.

Josef Hamacher

This character is a Reinforcement Reservist with a bristling beard who is a patient in the war hospital where Paul and Albert are brought with leg wounds. He tells a threatening hospital inspector that he himself threw a bottle actually hurled by Paul to make someone shut the door through which the needless sound of Litany is keeping patients awake. Asked later why he took the blame, Josef grins and says he has a head injury, which really is a "shooting license." It relieves him of responsibility for his actions.

Franz Wachter

An arm-wound patient in the war hospital. His purpose in this story is to bring home to the reader the terrifying neglect of which helpless patients are sometimes victims. When he suffers a hemorrhage, his companions, all unable to walk, think their rings will never be answered. Also, Wachter introduces us to the Dead Room, from which no man returns.

Peter

Another patient, he has a serious lung injury. He is small, dark, curly-headed; he grows steadily worse and then is assigned to the Dead Room, which is conveniently near the mortuary. He cries out his unwillingness, but is pushed back on the stretcher. As they take him from the ward, he shouts his determination to return. To the amazement of all, he does.

Sister Libertine

Sister Libertine is a nurse who affords a pleasant contrast to unanswered bells, maliciously probing medics, and experimental surgeons who leave cripples in their wake. Her very presence brings cheer throughout the whole hospital wing.

Berger

Berger is a soldier who is killed as he tries to find and kill a suffering, wounded messenger dog. This character, as does Detering, illustrates in his demise how thin is the front-line soldier's assiduously developed but inherently artificial primitiveness. He limits his life to only those things most necessary in the trenches, and buries thoughts of all else. Occasionally, however, they come to life and disaster follows. In Detering's case, a cherry tree in bloom awakened them and brought him to a captured deserter's fate. Berger's buried feelings were aroused by a mere report of a wounded dog some two hundred yards away. He rushes blindly out of the trenches, but a pelvis wound interrupts his berserk errand of mercy.

ALL QUIET ON THE WESTERN FRONT

CRITICAL COMMENTARY

CRITICAL REACTION

Hailed almost immediately as the greatest war novel ever written, *All Quiet on the Western Front* was also the target of much criticism. Praise as well as criticism can be found in many of the reviews of the book on its publication. Discussion of some of these articles will be necessary in order to clarify Remarque's position as the modern Stephen Crane, a title bestowed upon him soon after the appearance of this book. Also necessary will be a brief comparison of his work with Crane's *The Red Badge of Courage*, as well as comment upon Remarque as an exception to the general rule in the history of German novelists.

PRAISE

Remarque has been called unique as a war novelist, without reservation, in such publications as *Book Review Digest*,

Booklist, The Saturday Review of Literature, Bookman, and *Catholic World.* Many other points of praise can be found there as well.

Remarque's novel has been called a work of art in which the horrors of war are described without a trace of political animosity or nationalism and with tremendous **realism**. He has been praised for a positive simplicity which borders on naivete, resulting not from too little experience, but from too much. *All Quiet on the Western Front* is compared also to an Ibsen tragedy in its lean savagery and is considered an indictment of war that would be overwhelming if one man could ever feel completely what another has suffered.

CRITICISM

On the other hand, disapproval was not completely without voice. Such criticisms are numerous in the publications already mentioned and are also answered there.

One criticism dealt with Remarque's "concentration." It was described as so sharp and bitter, so single and conclusive, as to cost the synthesis and conclusion demanded in any novel which otherwise could be called great. The rebuttal launched was that any sacrifice in scope was more than repaid by gain in strength and directness. Defenders claimed that, if not great, Remarque's work possessed a nearly perfect uniqueness, and they put forward the additional view that it had suffered from suppression and from deletion in translation.

Another charge was that color and scope are sacrificed in *All Quiet on the Western Front* to economic design, trenchant utterance, and episodic compactness. This time the defense stated that the almost impossible fusion of war's minutiae into narrative was worth all the sacrifice of color and scope.

To another accusation that Remarque's book lacked rhetoric and analysis, the rebuttal was an argument that both these qualities had to be sacrificed. The magnitude of the horror described would have rendered both rhetoric and analysis inadequate. They are properly replaced by a terrible simplicity that could never have been attained without experience long enough to make the unspeakable commonplace and whose analysis should have been all but meaningless to those outside the experiences described.

A final charge of sensationalism and brutality is simply shrugged off with the statement that no argument that Remarque wrote solely to shock or sell could possibly stand after a reading of the novel. The latter is proof per se that *All Quiet on the Western Front* is the product of suffering-not of trickery.

EXCEPTION TO THE GERMAN RULE

Whether or not Remarque's book rises above every criticism is a matter of opinion. So too is any assertion that it is an exception to the historical role of the German novel. Yet there is evidence to be found that it might have earned itself such a place if we look for the evidence in Roy Pascal's work, *The German Novel*. The novel has always been one of the more difficult media for German artistic expression. Writers in that country, even when romanticists, always had difficulty in concentrating upon manners, customs, usage, habit, and form in an effort to picture the external world as it was. Instead they chose to concentrate, as Pascal writes in *The German Novel* on "... inner transcendental values at the expense of outer social reality."

As a result, there were no characters and situations such as were found in the novels appearing in other countries. Later, in the modern period, we can find exceptions to this rule, but even in the case of the two most prominent, Kafka and Mann, the road from subjectivity to objectivity was difficult. In Kafka's case, for example, the outer world is indeed described objectively. But the picture so drawn of it is harsh, cruel, and hopeless, and corresponds all too closely to the inner world of Kafka's own soul, which is also presented.

In some ways Remarque's book may seem to fall into this pattern of lingering subjectivity. A closer examination, however, reveals that it does not.

The world of the front, for instance, is pictured as hopeless, subjective, though that description may seem. But how could it have been described otherwise by a realist from any other country. Certainly no rosier outlook was presented to anyone viewing a performance of the English play, *Journey's End*, by Robert Cedric Sheriff.

Equally hopeless, and this time also subjective, was the future pictured for Paul. But again this hopelessness and subjectivity is limited to one character, or at least to his generation. The teenager, caught in this maelstrom, with studies uncompleted before terrifyingly accelerated maturity made them seem ridiculous, could not look forward to a return to a world where no wife, no children, and no work awaited him. But positive situations did exist for farmers Katczinsky and Detering, had the war ended a little earlier, before it killed one and broke the sanity of the other. And certainly it was not the case with the five-times wounded author, who himself returned to continuous employment and, after eleven years, to world fame.

Points of difference or exception to this difficult transition from subjectivity to objectivity are much more discernible in Remarque's case.

Almost unanimously, critics have hailed his ability to write objectively without trace of nationalism, political animosity, or even personal feeling. Even when an inner world is pictured, it seems most often that of a character, not of Remarque.

Also, far from the complexity common to most German novelists, he writes with a simplicity that lets the story tell itself. No attempt is made to analyze that which he regarded too great for analysis.

Finally, he does not resort to the expressionism that was the refuge of most German writers and artists in his period. For them, it was not a question of the impression the world made upon the mind; instead, it was the effect the mind made upon the external world. They pictured, in words, paint, or stone, their own inner impressions of man or scene, and if others, familiar with either, didn't recognize them, then the exterior appearance was a false one. The inner images remained real and true, needing only to be perceived and communicated.

Not so with Remarque, who used selection or detailed description to picture a front hailed instantly by veterans of both sides as the most accurate description, per se, ever presented.

COMPARISON WITH STEPHEN CRANE

Almost instantly, Remarque's novel was compared to *The Red Badge of Courage*, a book which, by its very existence, ridiculed all the romantic depictions of war that had preceded it.

Remarque himself was proclaimed "the modern Stephen Crane". A comparison of the two writers may produce a defense against the charges of shock and sensationalism levied against both.

In each case, the author's work was a powerful indictment of war. Each writer employed **irony** and **realism** in the forms of naturalism and impressionism. Finally, both writers made use of symbolism and contrast. Yet in many ways their writing is quite different.

Irony is found on different occasions in both books, but for crowning examples we need to go no farther than the title of each. "*The Red Badge of Courage*" was a wound received as a result of cowardice; and "*All Quiet on the Western Front*" described a day which constituted the final step in the inexorable destruction of a man.

Symbolism, too, can be cited in both books, but here a word of caution is required. Too often there is a desperate search by the reader for symbols that aren't there. Commonly, symbolism is simply regarded as literary employment of fancy and **imagery**. Upon other occasions it is used to represent abstraction. Finally, in its narrow sense, it constituted a protest against **realism** by French writers of the late nineteenth century, men who preferred to suggest rather than employ detailed description.

The last kind need not concern a reader or either Crane of Remarque. Neither was averse to detailed description. Nor is there any problem connected with the first, for both their books abound in **imagery**. It is the second type which is difficult to recognize without a key. An example in Crane's novel would be sunlight, which always marked a day of triumph, and overcast gray skies, which seemed to accompany defeat.

Remarque is less oblique in one instance. The earth is not only a symbol of a protective mother to the soldier; it is so addressed by Paul in Chapter Four. Almost as easy to translate are the examples in **imagery** afforded by the front as a whirlpool sucking men to their destruction and the air as a life force that leaps at Paul. Not so clear are the examples of the cathedral and its gardens, recollected in flashes of explosives, the beauty of Nature on the moors of the training camp, and the thin, frozen sound of the violin in the prison confines at night.

Indeed, the cathedral and its gardens are more easily discernible as examples of contrast than they are as symbols. Both Remarque and Crane re adept at increasing effect by this device. The recollected peace of a cathedral only intensifies war's violence, in the first instance, even as war's stupidity is enhanced in the second by the beauty of heather moving under the painting breath of soldiers who are practicing destruction.

So too is the effect of the Youth's humiliation deepened in *The Red Badge of Courage* by the contrast of infantry speeding forward to battle and mule teams in wild retreat, while he stands on the sidelines, a part of the latter, but wishing his actions had earned him a place with the former.

Where the two writers are most nearly alike, however, and also most vulnerable to the unjust charges of sensationalism brought against both, lies in the degree of **realism** employed by each. Any shocking situation reported with realistic accuracy is bound to shock. But such a reporter is not guilty of sensationalism unless he intended it, and labored to insure the effect by the techniques within his power. This might be said to be true with Dreiser's compulsive, detailed description in *The Old Neighborhood*, or with Steinbeck's nauseating if graphically detailed description of the slaying of the buzzard in *The Red Pony*.

Halfway between all-out naturalism and the rosy **realism** of Howells lies the impressionism employed by Crane and Remarque. A reading of either makes it quite apparent that neither shared Howells's belief in the possibility of a **realism** that would bring no blush to a lady's checks. Yet in neither case does one feel an urgent search for every existing detail, no matter how unpleasant. Instead, in each instance, there is the selectivity that is characteristic of the impressionist who attains his realistic accuracy by focusing on one or more details. If, as is often the case, there are none but sensational or shocking ones as possible objects of focus, then the fault lies barely in the writers, if in them at all.

ALL QUIET ON THE WESTERN FRONT AS A NOVEL

The classification of Remarque's story as a novel is more easily made today than it would have been in the past, when plot was an essential criterion. Theoretically, a novel must have characterization and plot, but in modern times the importance of plot has dwindled as interest centers increasingly upon characterization. Indeed, writers have almost totally abandoned the concept of plot as a carefully planned structure, removal of any piece of which would bring collapse. For this conception, they have substituted simply the idea of conflict resulting in change, and this may be found in the most modern of novels, as well as in *All Quiet on the Western Front*. Certainly Paul and every other character in the war were in the most vital conflict of all. Theirs was not a comparatively innocuous clash between love and feud, as in *Romeo and Juliet*, or between honor and ambition, as in *Macbeth*. Instead, it was one between the instinct of self-preservation and death in the form of war; and certainly everyone was changed as a result.

Two other "musts" for the novel are imagination and a basis of experience. In these respects also, Remarque's work qualifies. Paul is not in any respect Remarque or any other real person. If he were, he would not seem real himself to us. As John P. Marquand declares in his preface to H. M. Pulham, *Esquire*," ... nearly every writer ... will tell you that no actual human being is convincing ... upon the printed page... . A successful character in a novel ... is a conglomerate, a combination of dozens of traits, drawn from experience with hundreds of individuals... ." The character is real, according to Marquand, only if he represents a familiar type. "If he were to step out of the pages into a room, he would be pathetically distorted."

However, if Remarque's characters are imaginary, both they and the story have their roots in an experience as terrifying as ever formed the basis of a novel. Let us not forget that their creator returned to the front four times after wounds received there, only to encounter a fifth, most serious of all. Also, during that interim he was gassed.

There are further classifications of the novel which might be discussed before identifying Remarque's work, since it has already been criticized upon the ground of synthesis or plot, as the latter is conceived in the former and more formal sense.

This literary form falls into two broad divisions: novels classified according to purpose, and those identified according to manner. Each of these groupings, however, is capable of several subdivisions.

Theoretically, novels grouped according to the purpose for which they were written may be regrouped under as many purposes as there are authors. This, however, would be too subjective a reclassification. For practical reasons, the subdividing is upon a much narrower scale.

Such a more limited classification of novels written for purpose would include those designed to: (1) entertain; (2) present a problem or thesis; (3) present a historical background.

On the other hand, novels classified according to manner or nature of writing are regrouped as romantic, realistic, impressionistic, and naturalistic. Examination eliminates Remarque's novel from some of these subgroupings, but qualifies it for more than one.

To begin, *All Quiet on the Western Front* has both purpose and manner. An examination in the light of subdivisions under Purpose would eliminate it from the first immediately. Remarque certainly did not write such a story primarily to entertain, as did Stevenson in Kidnapped or Dumas in The Three Musketeers. Yet, a word of caution is needed here. Any successful novelist has to entertain in the sense that he must hold interest. You cannot present a problem or teach history if your novel is put down not to be picked up again.

Classification under one of Purpose's two remaining subdivisions is less difficult. Certainly Remarque presents a problem. It is that of the existence of wars fought in the main by those who have no desire for them or understanding of their causes. Also, the novel is important historically as a dispassionate, objective and accurate picture by a first-hand observer of action in one of the world's greatest conflicts.

But general opinion seems to regard the author's primary purpose as not the imparting of historical data. Instead it was the indictment of war by picturing it realistically in all its filth, cruelty, and destruction. A glance at examples of each type seems to support such a view. Although far afield from either, *All Quiet on the Western Front* seems to more resemble an indictment of slavery, such as Uncle Tom's Cabin, than it does Lew Wallace's historical novel, Ben Hur.

Classification under the subdivisions of Manner resembles that just described under Purpose. Elimination is easy, but final selection less so. Remarque's novel is not a romantic one, in which the author may throw plausibility of motive and probability of plot to the winds. It is not far removed from real life. And even Remarque's most ardent admirer could not recommend it as an escape vehicle. But to fit under this subdivision of Manner it would have to possess all of these qualities.

Positive classification, on the other hand, is almost impossible. Is it realistic, impressionistic, or naturalistic? Certainly it is the first. To fall under either of the last two groupings, it would have to contain elements of the first. Both the latter endeavor to give the reader a realistic picture. None of the three are concerned with the bizarre and heroic, which absorb the romanticist. And neither is Remarque. Despite their points in common, however, all three of these schools also have characteristics which are different. Both the realist and the impressionist wish to present a true picture, for example, but the realist wishes you to see, where the impressionist demands that you feel. Again, both impressionist and naturalist demand the right of selection, regardless of reader sensitivity, but the naturalist alone stresses determinism and absence of guilt.

These similarities and distinctions may be brought out through a brief inspection of the development in America of all three; after which a final classification of Remarque's novel may become easier.

In its first stages, American **realism** was the realism of William Dean Howells. He abjured the mawkish, the sentimental, and the romantic, but was convinced that **realism** could be as inextricably linked to the "decent" as to the "indecent." In his opinion, it was more challenging to the author in the former case, for then the reader is not so easily enthralled, despite bad workmanship, as he so often is in the latter case. His **realism** was necessarily limited to the upper strata of society, the only one he knew. But his plots were always probable, and his writing revealed expert analysis of character and high skill in the revelation of motives.

Henry James carried **realism** further than Howells. Although limited, like Howells, to the upper classes, he differed from Howells in that he embraced rather than rejected French **realism** as well as Russian. Flaubert and Turgenev became not only his acquaintances but his models. Also, to quote editors Bradley, Beatty, and Long in Volume 2 (Revised) of *The American Tradition in Literature*, "he accepted ... the naturalists' concept of the novelist as the clinical researcher into life, but did not follow their unselective zeal to report everything observed; he admitted a measure of determinism, but rejected the pessimistic extreme according to which human character becomes the waif of chance." Also, in the same work we read that James "... offset his portrayals of the evil tendencies of life toward greed, treachery, and pathological dualism by the constant representation of innocence, lofty choices, and moral idealism."

Stephen Crane, although he was credited with the introduction of naturalism into this country, was more of an impressionist than a naturalist in the Dreiser sense. The difference is similar to that between the camera and the artistic painter. Like the painter, a writer in impressionism is more interested in features than details, effect than object, feeling than sight. Yet in their insistence upon right of selection, and their graphic description of features so selected, their resemblance to naturalism is confusingly close.

Theodore Dreiser was perhaps the first and certainly one of the most famous examples of complete naturalism in this country. In his writing is seen an almost compulsive inclusion of details and a fatalistic determinism which negated all feelings of guilt upon the part of his characters. Both of these qualities mark the true naturalist. Both were rejected by James and Howells. The second is absent in Crane and Remarque.

Both Crane and Remarque were objective in their description of war. Both were detailed in this description and both were graphic and often horrifying in their selection of features. Also, in each book, there was the element of determinism, inevitable in any story of soldiers at war. In no other situation are men so many pawns with all individual choice removed. To this extent, both their novels could be called naturalistic. But in each book, the protagonist feels guilt-Crane's Youth toward a truly brave man, whom he had deserted in the field, and Remarque's Paul toward the French printer he had stabbed to death in a shell-hole. Further, in both writers we see examples of purposeful selection rather than the detached scientific observation of the true naturalist.

An examination of the very openings of their respective novels may help stamp them as impressionists, with more concern for feeling than sight. In the first pages of *The Red Badge of Courage*, Crane establishes the excitement attendant upon rumored movement of troops. Remarque takes less than one page to register the rare contentment that spreads over well-fed soldiers who have had enough sleep. Both openings reveal inclusion of detail, but Remarque's is narrative, related from the opening sentence to the effect he wishes to achieve. No irrelevant description is tolerated. Crane, on the other hand, permits himself an opening paragraph of descriptive setting. Yet it is not the camera variety. The cold, the river, and enemy campfires are all given human qualities, which are felt as well as seen. Neither possesses the mass of scientifically observed detail present in the introductory paragraph of Dreiser's *The Old Neighborhood*, although that short story vehicle allowed him even less latitude than that permitted novelists Crane or Remarque.

True, there is naturalistic, detailed description to be found frequently in both novels. The deaths of Jim Conklin and Franz Kemmerich are enough to place Crane and Remarque, respectively, in this school. Nevertheless, in each case, even in these descriptions, we find differences. The movements selected by Crane are those which give the effect of weird rites or an impish dance on the part of a dying man. The feeling of weird horror aroused in the witnesses occupies the author more than the death itself in this instance. Similarly, although Remarque is equally detailed in describing the steps in life's exit from Kemmerich's body, he is even more effective in his indirect description. Paul's helpless rage is increased as much by the surgeon's callous indifference to one of five amputees as it is by his friend's dying. The impatient, covert glances of orderlies at the bed, soon to be emptied, are equally effective, although they would not register in the direct-camera inclusiveness of the naturalist. We must conclude therefore that Remarque's story was a novel written in the impressionistic manner for the purpose of presenting a problem.

CHARACTERIZATION

Since, in the modern novel, character has become more significant than plot, no discussion of Remarque's book would be complete without reference to the author's all-important ability to bring to life in print real people who are representative not only of their own time and place but of all humanity. The hundred or more ways in which a writer can do this cannot be considered here; but the broad approach may be mentioned, as well as the manner in which Remarque applies them.

TECHNIQUES

General divisions of the techniques of characterization include description-direct or indirect-formal analysis, narration of the character's action, and the cumulative method.

The first, and probably the most commonly employed by a majority of writers, is direct description of appearance, in which individual features are stressed. This, of course, is varied with indirect portrayal, in which the reader apparently is left to draw his own conclusions from facts supplied by the author. Actually the reader's will be those of the author, because of the author's particular selection and presentation of facts. In this type of static characterization, the facts supplied or described directly may include name, lineaments, habitual posture or expression, clothing, surroundings, occupation or profession.

Character analysis, on the other hand, concerns itself with motives behind the actions of people in a story. A broad classification of such motivations includes urges described as life, sex, worship, power, and social. Variations of each are too numerous for classification here. The first, or life urge, for example, includes drives for self-preservation resulting from hunger, fear, and self-defense.

Narration is another means of characterization frequently employed, especially in novels of action, as is *All Quiet on the Western Front*. The old adage about action speaking louder than words is especially true as a source of information about character.

Finally, in the cumulative method, the picture is drawn by sporadic strokes until a complete portrait appears.

It now remains to see how Remarque applies these techniques. A rereading of the very first chapter is revealing. There, direct and indirect description are blended with narration. This is not the time to observe the cumulative method but we see the beginning of it in Kropp's case and we know that it will also be true in regard to Tjaden. Kropp is described directly as the clearest thinker in the group, and this is immediately supported by a narration which tells us he was first to be made lance-corporal. Again, narration reveals his incisiveness as he speaks bluntly and to the point to the orderly. This is repeated, as Kropp suddenly characterizes all the indifferent dressing-station staff as "damned swine." We see further justification later in the story when he brings Paul out of shock with his remarks about the sharp-shooting Sergeant Oellrich and their application to Paul's situation.

Muller on the other hand, is the subject of no direct description. We do not know what he looks like, but we draw a clear picture of his personality from the facts fed to us. He possesses foresight. This is made clear by direct statement and continually supported by narration. He brings a washbasin to the mess turned by circumstances into a windfall. And he realizes that Kemmerich's boots must go to someone. Accordingly, he manages so that someone will be he and not the orderly.

Tjaden's character comes through to us by both direct description and narration. He is that comparative rarity, a skinny glutton. Later, through the cumulative method of characterization, we get a complete picture of an elemental character who can be ferociously vindictive when humiliated and who possesses a primitive directness, hard to answer in debate. This is accompanied by a surprisingly acute sense of humor. But in addition, he has a crudeness which makes his absence desirable on the visit to the French girls.

In the opening chapter, Katczinsky appears most clearly of all, with the possible exception of Leer. We see him as a "shrewd, cunning and hard-bitten" forty-year-old farmer, "...with a face of the soil, bent shoulders, and a remarkable nose for dirty weather... ." Later, of course, his character becomes much more complete through continued narration.

Leer, seen more clearly than any save Katczinsky, is also the object of direct description. The two individual features stressed in his case are a full beard and a preference for girls from officers' brothels. We learn later that he is an excellent mathematician and, unlike Tjaden, a distinct asset on the visit to the house across the river, where he makes a tremendous hit with the blonde.

Kemmerich, in his dying condition, is, of course, the object of the most direct description of all. We see his emaciated figure and during narration we almost hear his panting breath. Other examples of direct description in the first chapter are the two cooks, red-headed Heinrich and fat Bulcke, and "… active little …" Kantorek with his "… grey tail-coat …" with "… a face like a shrewmouse." All others appearing there are described indirectly. There is Paul, already pictured as analytical, protective, tactful, and obviously a leader, although he never mentions this last characteristic in connection with himself.

Also, there is Haie Westhuis, whose hugeness is suggested by the statement that he can hide a ration-loaf in his hand. Then comes Detering, a peasant, like Kat, but whose face remains a blank to us. Not so his character, however. Something of that is revealed when we learn that he thinks only of his wife and farm. Finally, there is the excellent company commander, Bertinck, whose face is also unrevealed, but whose fairness, quiet leadership, and understanding come through to us in narration.

One of these, however, Heinrich, is the subject of more than direct description. He, by his own very character, creates the action in the first half of this story, and narration reveals in him the cowardice and contemptible meanness which almost precipitated what Paul would have described as a "dust-up."

An example of the final class of characterization, that of analysis, is presented to the reader by Remarque in the person of Corporal Himmelstoss. That former postman in civilian life has Kropp, Muller, Kemmerich, and Paul in his platoon at the Klosterberg training camp where he is the strictest disciplinarian of all the noncommissioned officers. Taking a special dislike to these four, he reveals his sadistic nature in meeting out to them almost inconceivably humiliating and painful duties. These tasks are so severe that they even meet with the disapproval of the German military system, and Himmelstoss is reprimanded on one occasion by a lieutenant. Now, long after escape from and even revenge on the little corporal, his former victims try to analyze him as they sit in the trenches. Convinced that Himmelstoss must have been quite different in civilian life, Paul wonders audibly how he happened to become so bullying a noncommissioned officer. Strangely enough, it is not the analytical Kropp, but the former farmer, Kat, who provides the explanation. He agrees roughly that Kropp's and Paul's explanation of the uniform and chain of command is correct, but says that the true answer goes deeper than that. He likens civilian officers unused to authority to a dog conditioned to eat potatoes. Reminding his audience that such a conditioned dog will snap at offered meat, he declares that men unused to authority will also snap at power when more than they are accustomed to is given them. Himmelstoss, and all other civilian officers, to more or less extent, are examples under Kat's theory, of the power urge in an extreme form.

STATIC CHARACTERS

There are three classes of characters in most stories. First come those acted upon by the chain of events and who grow or deteriorate as a result. Adam Bede would be an example of the former and Macbeth of the latter. Second come those individuals who by their very character create action, instead of being affected by it. The malicious Iago would be an outstanding example here, but the insanely jealous Othello and incredibly naive Desdemona were his aides. Finally, we have the static character who neither creates a story nor is influenced by it. Even Scott's heroes were of this type, but usually they have minor roles or are found in comedies or stories of the mystery type, where plot is the chief source of interest. Some of this type are to be found in *All Quiet on the Western Front* and this study can be completed with a brief discussion of them.

Among those with brief parts to play in this story, but who neither contribute to nor are changed by it, are Bulcke-whose only purpose is to bring out Ginger's cowardice by contrast. Another is the Russian prisoner-violinist -there, apparently, only to offer an opportunity for some beautiful writing. Sergeant Oellrich is a third, his role being confined to that of catalytic cure for Paul. And a fourth can be found in Sister Libertine, who is limited to providing background, albeit a cheerful one, in the otherwise horrifying hospital. Two final characters to be included in this class are Erna, Paul's elder sister, and Heinrich Bredmeyer, whose only act was to spread truthful bad news of the front.

None of these are vital to the story in that they contribute in any way to the vital **theme**, which is the transformation of Paul. They have no such roles as Kantorek, who betrayed him, Himmelstoss, so influential in his and others' military transformation from man to beast, Kat, who replaced Kantorek as Paul's true teacher, or Kropp, the closet remaining friend of his former civilian life. Neither do they contribute to the story, even in a minor way as do Heinrich, Josef Behm, the Little Brunette, or even Duval, the compositor who died without a single word of dialogue.

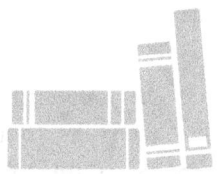

ALL QUIET ON THE WESTERN FRONT

ESSAY QUESTIONS AND ANSWERS

Question: How did Remarque use impressionism to draw a realistic picture of hopelessness in the Russian prison camp?

Answer: Three types of realistic writing are the rosy **realism** of William Dean Howells, the naturalistic, almost compulsive inclusion of details, usually unpleasant, which characterized the writings of Theodore Dreiser, and the impressionism of Remarque himself and Stephen Crane.

The first required plausibility of motive and probability of plot; but after that limited itself to accurate description only of those details which were neither shocking nor even unpleasant.

In the second instance, all details, no matter how repugnant, had to be pictured with meticulous accuracy. Also, added to this, was the element of determinism, which deprived characters of any degree of voluntary action and absolved them from all feelings of guilt.

Finally, in the case of impressionism, a realistic overall impression is created by accurate focus upon a few details neither necessarily pleasant nor unpleasant, but necessary to the telling of the story and to the issue. This was the technique of Remarque in *All Quiet on the Western Front* when he pictured the quiet despair of the Russian prison camp. He concentrated upon such details, or even the absence of them, as food held silently before starving eyes, absence of former flashing knives, disease-stained clothes and mournful nocturnal music. The result is an overall impression of prison's capacity of drain from its inmates all manhood, strength, hope, and even resentment. It is realistic and grim, and as moving as any detailed description could hope to be.

Question: Did Remarque sacrifice conclusion to concentration in this novel?

Answer: Neither critic nor supporter could deny the remarkable power of concentration revealed by Remarque in *All Quiet on the Western Front*. Equally true is that concentration on any object in artistic fields always carries with it a potential for elimination. The painter eliminates time by concentrating on space even as the composer eliminates space in his concentration on time. However, conclusion in the dramatic novel where time is limited is not the same as conclusion in the chronicle type of novel, which is written against a background of change itself, or rather life in perpetual change.

In such writing, probably the greatest example of which is Tolstoy's *War and Peace*, characters may not pick the time of death demanded by artistic conclusion in a dramatic novel, as did Captain Ahab in *Moby Dick*. Instead they may die, apparently without reason, as did Tolstoy's Prince Andrew, even as he was making plans for his future. But this cannot be called a faulty conclusion in the chronicle, where fate cannot be known, as it always is in the dramatic novel. In the chronicle type of writing, which Remarque's work resembles, as does Crane's, life is not limited to a single character, nor does it end with his death. Rather, we have the story of birth, death, and rebirth.

Crane writes not a story of one youth but of all youth in war- naturally cowardly, but capable of heroism, and with a potential for swinging back and forth between the two extremes for all time. So too, the last paragraph of Remarque's novel conveys more than the death of a single soldier struck down with no preparation, even as we were facing with him a post-war life that would have made this unexpected death desirable, Instead we are made to see an entire generation whose physical survival is a matter of complete chance but whose doom is certain.

Question: Does *All Quiet on the Western Front* suffer from lack of plot and characterization?

Answer: If a story is to be called a plotted novel rather than a simple narrative with no claim to greatness, every incident is essential. Its removal would cause more than a mere gap but a collapse of the whole. Is this true in the case of *All Quiet on the Western Front*? Does this story spring from a series of planned connected incidents and from the interaction upon one another of characters set down in this chain of events? Does it lead up to a **climax** and then descend logically and gracefully to an artistic conclusion? Or do we simply witness the gradual destruction of youth by the war machine, even as we might witness the stages in the demolition of a building as it could be brought to us by a master of summary, scene, and description?

Each side can be argued. Certainly, there is a **climax** in this story. In successive stages Paul suspects that there will be no return for him, even though he should survive the war. But conviction and **climax** come on his visit home during leave.

Also there is characterization, sometimes broad, occasionally brief, but usually vivid. The cowardly cook, the splendid company commander, the contemptible corporal of the training camp, and the arrogant major encountered on leave are all real people to the reader. Also, in some cases, they are in themselves responsible for the action of the story. Paul and his schoolmates would not have enlisted were it not for their headmaster, later a ridiculous figure upon the moor. Nor, except for him, should one of them have died so soon. In general, however, characterization has nothing to do with action here as it does in other great works of fiction. Iago, in Othello, for example, could have accomplished nothing without Othello's potential for homicidal jealousy and Desdemona's almost incredible naivete. But here the stage was set for these boys long before they cidal jealously and Desdemona's almost incredible naivete. But here the stage was set for these boys long before they were born, when an Iron Chancellor paved the way for a Prussian military machine, and then, like Frankenstein, let the monster break from his control. Neither are the incidents linked in an interdependent pattern. Kantorek's ferocious patriotism, the cruelty of Himmelstoss, Bulcke's stinginess, and the death of Kemmerich are all incidents contributing to action, but disconnected ones. They do not follow in planned development as do the feud, edict against further fighting, insult, duel, and death of Tybalt, which led up to the **climax** in *Romeo and Juliet*. Nevertheless, despite their lack of connection and their capability of omission, with only resultant gaps rather than collapse, these incidents are presented by Remarque with a selection and narrative power that gives us an unforgettable impression of war's power to destroy even its survivors.

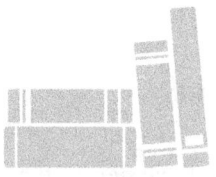

BIBLIOGRAPHY

OTHER WORKS OF REMARQUE

Arch of Triumph. Translated from the German by Walter Sorell and Lindley Denver. New York; Appleton-Century Crofts, 1945. (A German refugee doctor falls in love with an actress in Paris, just before World War II.)

Spark of Life. Translated from the German by James Stern. New York: Appleton-Century Crofts, 1952. (In this book Remarque draws a somber and terrifying picture of a German concentration camp.)

A Time to Love and a Time to Die. Translated from the German by Lindley Denver. New York: Harcourt, Brace & World, 1954. (A young German soldier and his sweetheart try to forget World War II during his three-week furlough. Praised for its balance of simple **theme** and restrained, unpretentious treatment, the novel's high point is considered to be the portrayal of life in a city ruined by war. Nevertheless, Robert Gorham David declared in *The New York Times* that "... The inner realities do not measure up to the outer ones. Instead of being made more intense and complex by the violence which surrounds it, the love affair takes on some of the unrealistic city itself, seen at night with only the moon to light it."

CRITICAL COMMENTARY

Booklist 25 (1929), 369. (A discussion of the concentration of material in Remarque's work and the strength and direction resulting from such concentration.)

Bookman 69 (July, 1929), 552. (In this issue, *All Quiet on the Western Front* was called a work of art possessing " ... the lean savagery of an Ibsen tragedy... ")

Book Review Digest (1929). (Remarque is praised for his lack of passion and anger as he wrote a powerful indictment against war.)

Catholic World 130 (1929). (This issue justifies Remarque's abandonment of rhetoric and analysis in describing a situation too great for either.)

The New York Times (June 2, 1929). (Remarque is defended against charges of brutality and sensationalism.)

Pascal, Roy. *The German Novel*. Toronto: Manchester University Press, 1956 (A description of the difficulties of the novel as a medium of art in Germany.)

OTHER WORKS FOR STYLISTIC COMPARISON WITH REMARQUE

Crane, Stephen. *The Red Badge of Courage*. New York: Harcourt, Brace & World, 1962. (In this book are found examples of the techniques of irony, **realism**, naturalism, and impressionism which both Crane and Remarque employed to indict war.)

Dreiser, Theodore. *The Old Neighborhood*, Chains. New York: New York World, 1927. (An outstanding example of naturalistic, compulsive, detailed description, found much more often in Dreiser than in Crane or Remarque)

Steinbeck, John. *The Red Pony*. New York: Viking Press, 1937. (In this story can be found the type of naturalistic inclusion of unpleasant details deemed unnecessary by William Dean Howells in his interpretation of realism.)

HISTORICAL BACKGROUND

Waterhouse, Gilbert. *A Short History of German Literature*. London: Methuen, 1962. (This work describes the type of expressionism in which many writers - but not Remarque - sought refuge in postwar Germany.)

Gooch, George P. *Germany*. New York: Charles Scribner's Sons, 1925. (This history of Germany gives us a clear picture of the development of the Prussian militarism that resulted in World War I.)

Crutwell, C.F. *A History of the Great War*. London: Oxford University Press, 1934. (Crutwell discusses the terrifying superiority of weapons and materiel over the individual which characterized World War I.)

www.ingramcontent.com/pod-product-compliance
Lightning Source LLC
LaVergne TN
LVHW011739060526
838200LV00051B/3253